EXTREME SPORTS
MOTOCROSS

by Tracy Vonder Brink

pogo

Ideas for Parents and Teachers

Pogo Books let children practice reading informational text while introducing them to nonfiction features such as headings, labels, sidebars, maps, and diagrams, as well as a table of contents, glossary, and index.

Carefully leveled text with a strong photo match offers early fluent readers the support they need to succeed.

Before Reading

- "Walk" through the book and point out the various nonfiction features. Ask the student what purpose each feature serves.
- Look at the glossary together. Read and discuss the words.

Read the Book

- Have the child read the book independently.
- Invite them to list questions that arise from reading.

After Reading

- Discuss the child's questions. Talk about how they might find answers to those questions.
- Prompt the child to think more. Ask: Would you like to try motocross? Why or why not?

Pogo Books are published by Jump!
5357 Penn Avenue South
Minneapolis, MN 55419
www.jumplibrary.com

Copyright © 2025 Jump!
International copyright reserved in all countries.
No part of this book may be reproduced in any form without written permission from the publisher.

Library of Congress Cataloging-in-Publication Data

Names: Vonder Brink, Tracy, author.
Title: Motocross / by Tracy Vonder Brink.
Description: Minneapolis, MN: Jump!, Inc., [2025]
Series: Extreme sports | Includes index.
Audience: Ages 7–10
Identifiers: LCCN 2024030333 (print)
LCCN 2024030334 (ebook)
ISBN 9798892136365 (hardcover)
ISBN 9798892136372 (paperback)
ISBN 9798892136389 (ebook)
Subjects: LCSH: Motocross—Juvenile literature.
Sports sciences—Juvenile literature.
Classification: LCC GV1060.12 .V66 2025 (print)
LCC GV1060.12 (ebook)
DDC 796.7/56—dc23/eng/20240701
LC record available at https://lccn.loc.gov/2024030333
LC ebook record available at https://lccn.loc.gov/2024030334

Editor: Alyssa Sorenson
Designer: Molly Ballanger
Content Consultant: Derek Dauer

Photo Credits: HStarr/iStock, cover; Anthony Aneese Totah Jr/Dreamstime, 1; stockphoto-graf/Shutterstock, 3; Warren Price Photography/Shutterstock, 4; Andrei Metelev/iStock, 5; Pukhov K/Shutterstock, 6-7; Holubtsov Vitalii/Shutterstock, 8-9; Real Sports Photos/Shutterstock, 10; Tomasz Boinski/Shutterstock, 11; Wirestock Creators/Shutterstock, 12-13; Kirkam/Shutterstock, 14-15; tarczas/Shutterstock, 16-17; Cal Sport Media/Alamy, 18; Bryan Lynn/Icon Sportswire/Getty, 19; OlegRi/Shutterstock, 20-21; Krutov Igor/Shutterstock, 23.

Printed in the United States of America at Corporate Graphics in North Mankato, Minnesota.

TABLE OF CONTENTS

CHAPTER 1
Gear Up 4

CHAPTER 2
Let's Race! 10

CHAPTER 3
Best of the Best 18

ACTIVITIES & TOOLS
Try This! 22
Glossary 23
Index 24
To Learn More 24

CHAPTER 1
GEAR UP

Motocross riders race into a corner. They pass one another. Number 67 takes the lead!

track

Motocross is a type of motorcycle race. Riders race around a dirt track. It has corners and jumps.

CHAPTER 1 | 5

A motocross bike's **frame** is built to handle jumps and bumps. The bike is powered by an engine. It burns gasoline. This turns parts inside the engine. A rider twists the throttle. This sends more gasoline to the engine. The bike goes faster!

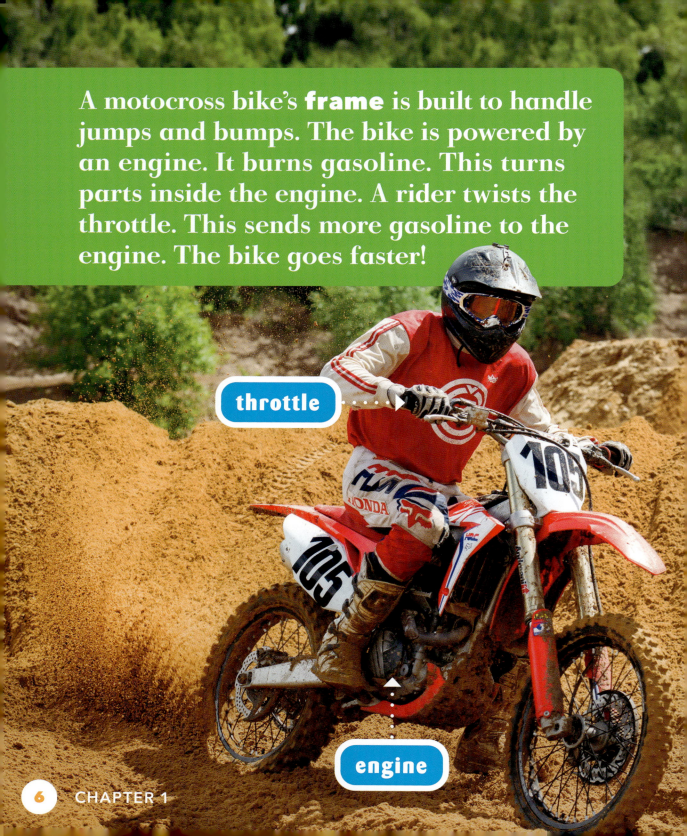

throttle

engine

TAKE A LOOK!

What are the parts of a motocross bike? Take a look!

The rider pushes the shift lever up with their foot. The bike **shifts** into a higher **gear**. The wheels spin faster. Up a hill, the rider shifts down to a lower gear. The bike has more power to climb.

If the rider is going too fast, they squeeze the brake lever. Brake pads push against a part attached to the wheels. This creates **friction**. It slows the wheels.

DID YOU KNOW?

Motocross riders are fit. Why? They need to be strong to control the bike.

CHAPTER 1

CHAPTER 2
LET'S RACE!

Riders line up at the starting gate. They lean forward on their bikes. Why? Putting more weight on the front wheel helps it grip the ground better. The gate drops. The bikes **accelerate**. The race begins!

gate

Racers ride their bikes up a small hill. The hill acts as a ramp. Ramps help riders **launch** their bikes into the air! **Gravity** pulls the bikes back to the ground.

gravity

CHAPTER 2

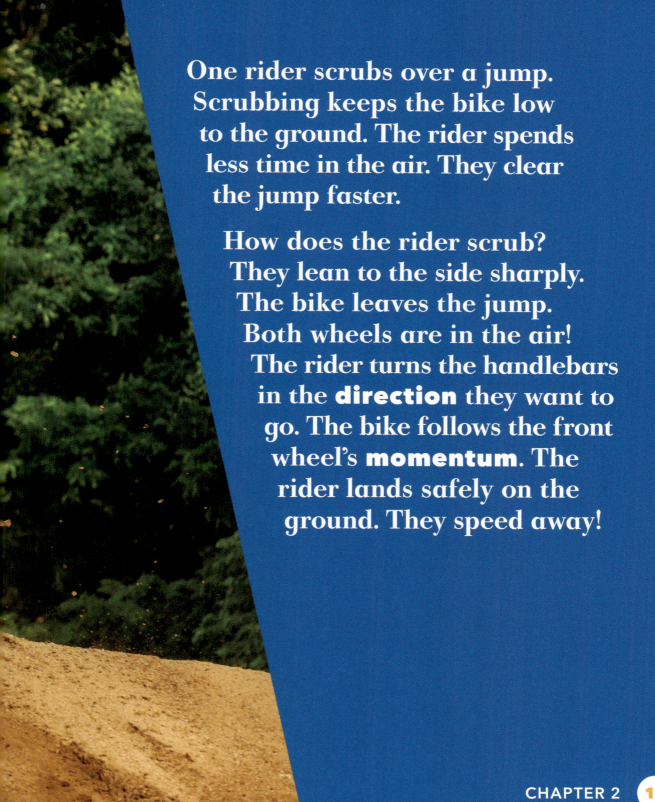

One rider scrubs over a jump. Scrubbing keeps the bike low to the ground. The rider spends less time in the air. They clear the jump faster.

How does the rider scrub? They lean to the side sharply. The bike leaves the jump. Both wheels are in the air! The rider turns the handlebars in the **direction** they want to go. The bike follows the front wheel's **momentum**. The rider lands safely on the ground. They speed away!

Next is the whoop section. This is a row of bumps. Racers ride their bikes on top of the bumps. Why? Riding in a straight line on top is faster than going up and down the bumps.

A rider makes a sharp right turn. They lean their body to the left. Why? This keeps the bike balanced. It does not tip over. The finish line is in sight!

DID YOU KNOW?

Riders can crash. Gear helps. Helmets protect riders' heads. Chest and back protectors help, too. They spread out any **impact**. This helps prevent injury.

CHAPTER 2   17

CHAPTER 3
BEST OF THE BEST

Some of the best riders **compete** in the Pro Motocross Championship. They race in 11 events around the United States.

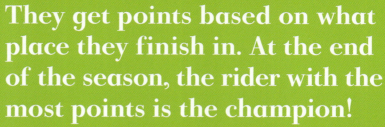

They get points based on what place they finish in. At the end of the season, the rider with the most points is the champion!

CHAPTER 3 19

Fast bikes and **physics** help motocross racers win. They race to be the best. They have fun, too!

> **DID YOU KNOW?**
>
> Mud does not stop a motocross rider. Races are held rain or shine!

CHAPTER 3

ACTIVITIES & TOOLS

TRY THIS!

ANGULAR MOMENTUM TEST

Angular momentum helps keep objects, such as wheels, spinning. Explore how it works with this fun activity!

What You Need:
- a plastic water bottle
- water

1. Fill the bottle full of water. Screw on the lid.
2. Toss the bottle in the air. How quickly does the bottle spin? Toss it harder. Can you make it spin faster?
3. Pour out water so one-third is left in the bottle. Screw on the lid.
4. Toss the bottle in the air again. Watch how quickly it spins. Does it go faster or slower than the full bottle? Toss it harder. Can you make it spin faster?
5. How does the amount of water change how the bottle spins? How do you think this applies to motocross bikes?

GLOSSARY

accelerate: To go faster.

compete: To try to win a contest.

direction: The course something is moving toward.

frame: The main structure of a motocross bike that holds it together and supports the bike parts and rider.

friction: The force that slows down objects when they rub against each other.

gear: One of the toothed wheels that works together with other parts to change the speed of a vehicle.

gravity: The force that pulls things toward the center of Earth and keeps them from floating away.

impact: The action of one object hitting another with force.

launch: To throw forward.

momentum: The force or speed something gains as it moves.

physics: The science that deals with matter, energy, and their interactions.

shifts: Changes gears.

ACTIVITIES & TOOLS 23

INDEX

accelerate 10
brake lever 7, 9
corner 4, 5
engine 6, 7
frame 6
friction 9
gasoline 6
gate 10
gravity 11
handlebars 13
helmets 17
hill 9, 11
injury 17
jumps 5, 6, 13
launch 11
momentum 13
physics 20
Pro Motocross Championship 18
ramp 11
scrubs 13
shift lever 7, 9
throttle 6, 7
track 5
whoop section 14

TO LEARN MORE

Finding more information is as easy as 1, 2, 3.
1. Go to www.factsurfer.com
2. Enter "motocross" into the search box.
3. Choose your book to see a list of websites.